Messages for Mom

Fran Banting

DEDICATION

To all the children who have fallen into the grips of addiction and the
Moms who continue to stand by their sides.

CONTENTS

To my husband, Terry.

Our life path may have some obstacles and detours along the way
but our joys and successes make the journey so much more fun.

PREFACE

I think I must have grown up in a bubble. I was raised in a normal family with a normal upbringing. I always saw the good in people, never had any fears, and thought that evil only existed in the movies. I guess you could say I saw the world with rose colored glasses.

Then I grew up.

I seemed to find out the hard way that there were awful things that happened in reality, I just hadn't experienced them yet. There were the usual things that were shocking, such as sudden deaths, car accidents, and illnesses, but nothing blindsided me more, than discovering my child had an addiction.

I think the reason was that I was never exposed to alcohol and drugs growing up. Oh sure, there were the high school experiments with friends, but I never really enjoyed the feelings I had, especially when hungover the next day. I had more productive things to do than spend my day with a dehydrated brain. I seem to need every brain cell to be active for me to function in my life.

Maybe I'm a prude. I don't know. I don't drink. I don't smoke. I pay my bills on time. I have no speeding tickets. I'm as straight as an arrow. I try to do everything right, following the rules of life, do unto others as you would have done to yourself. So, if I'm doing everything right, how could something go so wrong?

What was so unnerving about addiction, is that it was happening right under my nose and I didn't see it, mainly because I didn't know what it looked like. I was totally blindsided.

I didn't know that there were functioning addicts living in the world. I assumed they were all in alleys and on the streets.

Could people actually have an addiction and lead a normal purposeful life? Yes, they can, and they do. The only difference between them and I is that they are high. Yeah, I was caught way off guard.

Like any Mom, I went into full gear to help my child, after all, I am Mom and I can fix anything, right?

Funny thing about people. They think they can take charge and just change another person. The only person anyone can change is themselves. I know this all too well. As a Holistic Life Coach, I preach this philosophy all day long. I know that to ignite any change around you, you have to start with yourself.

I knew that I was powerless to do anything about my child, but I could go full board with myself. So, I got to work on me.

I realized that if anything was going to happen, it had start right in my own home. We had to work from the inside out. It wasn't an easy journey, and I'm well aware that it is never ending, but we took those first few steps and the changes started to happen.

Along the way I discovered a lot of things about our situation. Resources were few, options for my child were few, and that no one in this world cared. Sitting back and waiting to be saved by someone or something was not going to happen. We had to work together as a family and save ourselves.

More surprising to me was that there were so many Moms in the same situation, who were looking for outside resources to help them on their journey.

Through various meetings and groups, I saw these Moms struggle as they were waiting for some miracle, not realizing that they could get the ball rolling right here and now in their own homes.

I wanted Moms who had a child with an addiction to know that they could take control of themselves and their environments, and start to ignite change, if anywhere, in themselves.

As I began to share my story with friends, strangers and anyone who would listen, I saw just how rampant this problem was, not just in our community, but across the nation.

I was not alone!

Many Moms are suffering along with their children as they face the horrible illness of addiction.

When you take the stigma and shame that is added to the stress and anxiety that comes with dealing with a child's addiction, sometimes it is more than a Mom can take.

The good news in all of this, is that Moms are strong and powerful. Moms are capable of things that other mortal humans will ever know. Moms have the abilities and foresight to make great things happen.

When Mom changes, so does everything around her.

I wrote "Messages for Mom" to help my fellow Moms get through one of the most difficult situations they may face in their lives. It is to help them get back control of themselves, their minds, and their lives.

They just need to know how to tap into their inner strength and release their power.

More importantly there is one thing Moms who have a child with an addiction need to know.

They are not alone!

Fran Banting

Chapter 1

I AM MOM

Hey, Mom.

Here you are! That great person that has earned the title of Mom! Isn't it a great title? Congratulations!

Did you know that many people go their entire lives never being able to achieve the ultimate goal of becoming a mother? But you did it. You had a child and not only do you adore them, they mean the world to you.

You did it, and you are, Mom! That title was well earned, and well deserved. You worked hard for it, didn't you?

The bond between mother and child, well, nobody understands it, so how can someone possibly explain it? Only you can because you have been there for every step. The amazing birth of your child. The child that you attained by dreaming of wanting and having it, and the next thing you know there it is in your arms. Such a gift, the gift of life. It was that day that you committed to loving and caring for this child for the rest of your life. That love is undeniable. Who could possibly understand that bond other than a mother?

You share a similarity with all other mothers in this world. They all know the magic of motherhood. But you have one thing they will never attain. No other mother in the world knows your child the way you do. Only you and your child know the special bond that exists. That is because it is a special connection that is formed only through mother and child. And you are the only person in the Universe that has this bond with your child. No one can give it to you, and no one can take it away. It is your and your child's exclusive right until the end of time. There is only one Mom and that is you for this child.

You have been assigned the title. What an honor and privilege to be Mom.

There is also one more special thing that came with your child, and that is the invisible umbilical cord that keeps you and your child connected. That force that no one else can feel but you, Mom. All you have to do is to look into that child's eyes and you could feel that love connection, without words, without touching, without anything except that invisible bond. Mom and child.

Remember your first years with your baby? Such a perfect being! Every time you coddled and looked at them you would dream about how they would grow up to be so happy and successful. You wanted only the best for them.

You saw them taking on the world each day, with so many dreams, and you went along side for the ride. You did your best to give them everything they needed to grow up into a happy and successful human being!

It didn't matter if it was a slow methodical journey or a long, hard difficult one, once you had that child in your arms, the world changed for you, didn't it? And with that came your hopes and dreams of what their life was going to look like as they grew up, and what part you were going to play in that life.

Remember all the times they ran to you whenever they were scared or hurt, and there you were with open arms ready to nurture. You always had all the answers. You are Mom! And if anything came near them that would hurt or harm them, there you were. Mama Bear!

You had a strength that even surprised yourself. You were always there for them. The protector. You are Mom! All of your selfless acts, no matter how tired, how against it, or how for it, you did what you had to do for them to be happy. Your child was always put first. You worked tirelessly for them to have all that they needed. Mom, you are so amazing!

All of the ways that you showed up, with your love, your hugs and kisses, and telling them how special they were and the things you did to prove your love to them. Mom was always there.

You were there for all of the firsts. The first tooth, the first steps, the first day of school, their first loves, the first friends, the first teachers. All of their new experiences, you both rolled with it. Some were good, some were bad.

You both discovered how to work through any experience together, didn't you? Each problem, each issue, positive or negative, was new territory for the two of you, but you both learned and walked through it together. Sometimes easily, sometimes with some work.

Mom! You were the one with all the answers! Even when you didn't know what to do, you found out and made sure your child got what they needed. Even when sometimes you felt like you had nothing left. No more energy, no more time, no more money. You found a way. You are Mom. That force!! That power!!

And your child knows it! You are their only mother. There only is one, true Mom. And that's you! No one can know the bond that you share with your child, the love, the pain, the connection.

You always had what they needed to get by. You still do. You are still that Mom. I need you to know it!! I need you to own it!! I need you to say it and be it!! You are Mom!!

Sometimes it may feel like that connection is gone, but it is not. It is there, deep down, and you know it is there. And your child knows it's there. Just like when they were growing up. Mom was there then and she is here now. That power. That force.

You are like a beacon of hope. You are that majestic lighthouse in the distance seen through the thick fog and stormy waters. There you are standing strong and powerful against the winds, the water, and whatever else the world throws at it, but at all times, shining a light so powerful, that the smallest boat, caught in the biggest storm, can see your light.

You are still that beacon of hope, Mom. You are still the light that your child sees.

Your child is caught in one of the biggest storms of their life.

The direction to safety and comfort is your light, Mom. You may not feel it now, but you still are, Mom. You have more power than you know.

It's time to regain your place. Your dreams for your child have not died. They are still there. Of course, they are. That's why you are here, now, reaching out for an answer. An answer to the problem that both you and your child are facing.

It's time to face this experience head on. It's time for Mom to stand tall and gain some control.

I know you can do it, Mom. I know you don't feel like your light is very bright at the moment. Yes, you may have dimmed and faded, but you are ready to cast that light again, aren't you, Mom?

I know that right now it is dark, so, very dark. And the storm is so bad, so, so, very bad.

This is the biggest storm of your and your child's lives.

Your child is like a lost boat, in the dark, trying to weather the storm. They need to be moving in the right direction. Towards the beacon of hope. Can you be that light?

Mom, you may not be able to control the waves, the storm, or even save the boats in the water, but you can be that light that shows the way to safety and peace.

You are Mom!

Mom………let's get your light shining bright again!

"When we are no longer able to change a situation, we are challenged

to change ourselves."

Victor Frankl

Chapter 2

I AM AWARE

Hey Mom!

How are you doing today?

What's going on in your mind? Are you full of worry and doubt today? The, "What ifs?" Are you full of all those scary thoughts and scenarios that constantly play out in your mind? "What if this," and "What if that?"

I bet your imagination is pretty vivid as you replay all of those awful things that could be happening right now in your child's life. It's just another day with the same old thoughts and feelings, isn't it?

It's like you can almost predict the future in your mind of exactly what is going to happen. You can see it all so clearly. There in the middle of the darkness is your child…..trapped. You, there watching and not being able to save them. No matter how hard you try, it doesn't matter what you do or say, they are stuck in their nightmare.

How will they ever find their way out? Can't they see the danger right before their eyes? They are setting themselves up for a life of doom and danger. Why can't they see that they are the ones that need to pull themselves out? Why can't they just do it?

The continuous nightmare is looping in your mind.

You've never felt so helpless have you, Mom? I can almost bet that you know exactly how they feel. You can actually sense and feel exactly what they are feeling. Of course, you can. You are Mom! Only you can sense the danger they are in and feel what they are feeling. You are bonded.

With every day that they are disintegrating they are taking a part of you with them. Little by little, with each day that goes by, you become less of yourself as you move into their despair right alongside them.

There's that bond, loud and clear. You can feel what they feel. They are trapped and can't escape the danger. Of course, you know exactly what they need to do to get free. It all makes sense in your mind. You can see it so clearly. Just like before, you want to kick into Mom mode and save the day. But this time it is different, isn't it, Mom?

You want to just take control your child, stop their addiction, and help them move on with their life. But here you are…… helpless. You have no control! For the first time in your life you can't make it better. It is all in their hands. They are trapped and there is something stronger and darker than they can control and they cannot escape.

And just like them, you are trapped. There is something stronger and darker than what you can control and you cannot escape.

You know exactly what it feels like to be trapped, don't you? That is because your child is not the only one trapped in addiction.

Imagine this. Your child's first waking thought in the morning and every last thought before going to bed is their addiction. Nothing else. They are controlled and overpowered by the need and their thoughts are 100% revolving continuously around their addiction. They are stuck in the cycle. And it is this addiction that is destroying their minds, their bodies and their lives. And there you are Mom, with front row seats, having to endure seeing your child living a life you never would have imagined for them.

From the moment you wake up in the morning, to the end of the day when you lay your head down to rest, the first and last thoughts are always those of your child. Nothing else. You are controlled and overpowered by the negative and destructive thoughts of your child's situation.

You too are addicted. It is this addiction that is destroying your mind, your body and your life, isn't it, Mom?

Addiction has many forms.

Your child and their addiction are controlling your every thought, your every movement, your entire being.

You have taken every last breath, every last ounce of energy and used it all on the dark thoughts about your child. Just like an addiction. It is the first thing you wake up to, the thought of your child and their addiction, and it is the last thing you go to bed with. The thought of your child and their addiction.

You are trapped with this recurring nightmare in your mind and in your life. This is your life. Your days are spent thinking about your child, trying to find out where they are, what they are doing, because you must satisfy your need to know.

The addiction to your child and their addiction is slowly killing you. Day by day. It is chipping away at your dreams, your wants and needs, and your life. Thought by thought, each negative dark thought, strips you of life.

But, it's not always doom and gloom. Every once in a while, there is a bright light. You laugh at something funny, or a person, or a story, and you sense happiness again. For a brief moment you feel what it is like to enjoy something. A little glimmer of life, a little bit of love or positive feeling that is kind of warm and fuzzy. It brightens you and your day even if just for a brief moment, before the heaviness of your burden comes flowing back in and overtakes you again.

That little bit of light, that little brief moment of happiness and laughter, it felt so good. It took you from the darkness and into the light. That moment of removing your thoughts from the child and their addiction, it moved you a bit, didn't it, Mom?

It is possible. You can move yourself from that darkness to the light. It just takes one little thing.

One small distraction from the horror of your nightmares. For a brief moment you were awake and saw what it is like to live life with happiness. So, then this is proof, it is possible to move from the darkness into the light.

You know because you did it.

One small action. One small thought. One small event can move you closer to feeling what it is to be normal and smile. Could it happen? Could you move yourself from your own addiction of your child, to freedom?

Just think. If all it takes is one small positive action for you to feel happy again and move you out of the darkness, could that same small positive action maybe work for your child as well?

Perhaps.

Your entire life you have nurtured and cared for your child. Your child has always been front and center. But now you are out of control, trying to control something you have no control over. Your child's addiction. And your child is out of control, trying to control something they have no control over.

The only thing you can control right now is yourself.

It's time to put you front and center. You need to make the decision to move away from your addiction to your child, and to focus on you and your happiness.

Mom, you need to know what happiness feels like again. You need to come back to life. Your loved ones need to see Mom again. That light, that force. They all miss you and need your guidance.

What will turn on your light and allow you to release your brightness? What makes you happy that moves you into a wonderful positive state? Is it a video, a small affirmation, a hug from a friend or family member? Seek it out.

As you discover how to focus on yourself for positive change, and how to break free from your trap, others will be watching. You will be the guiding light on how to take control.

Forge the path Mom. It all starts with you.

Chapter 3

I WANT

Hey Mom,

Can you imagine just making a wish and having it come true?

If only you had a magic genie that could be summoned up to help you. It would be so great to just have to ask for what you want and to have it magically appear. Even if it was just one wish, wouldn't that be wonderful?

What if there was a such a magic way to get exactly what you want? What would you wish for?

I know you so well. I bet I could guess right now. You wouldn't wish for anything for yourself. You wouldn't wish for clothes, or money, or a new job. You wouldn't wish for a fancy car, a trip around the world or your dream home. You wouldn't wish for anything material or self-serving. You would make one wish. You would wish for your child to be happy and healthy and living a successful life, wouldn't you?

You are Mom! And for you, your child always comes first. You can't help it. It comes with the territory. That child is the most important thing that has ever come into your life, why would you change that now?

Remember those times when they were small and you would stare at them and wonder what they were going to grow up to be, who they would marry and what careers they would pursue? Remember those thoughts? Wasn't that fun? Those are great memories, aren't they?

When you thought about those things you felt good, didn't you? Dreaming, pretending. Just like a child dreams and pretends. You as a Mom did the same about your child. Sweet dreams.

Those wonderful, cherished dreams, and the amazing feelings that you would get when you thought that way, today seem so distant, almost unattainable. But are they really?

Your dreams all started in your mind. They weren't in your child's mind, or anyone else's, just in yours. You saw this wonderful image by bringing it up in your imagination. You brought up this idea or dream in your own mind.

No one put it there for you. Your mind just took you to this pretend world where your child was older and living the life of your dreams.

Dreams start in our minds with our imaginations. That is the ignition of any idea or dream.

Can you still dream, Mom? Can you still bring up wonderful images, happy images, or have you forgotten how to dream?

Maybe you used to dream when you were younger, you were sitting in class at school and you weren't particularly interested in what the teacher was saying. Off you went to dreamland, picturing something other than what was in front of you in reality. Or maybe it was when you would sleep in and lay in bed, just wondering about life, your future, and what you wanted to pursue.

Remember staring away and getting pulled into that dreamland where you would escape into a world that was fun and happy? Where did you go? What did you see?

And it wasn't just the dream that was important, it was the way it made you feel while you were dreaming. Do you remember that feeling? It was so exhilarating, wasn't it? Your whole body would react as you would play out this fantasy in your mind. It was like you were making it come to life and you were there in person actually living the dream.

Your whole body was absorbed in the thought. You were vibrating with love and happiness. Dreams have a way of making you react and come alive. They have the ability to awaken what is inside. Think about it, Mom.

How many of those dreams that you had in your past have actually come true? Have you ever thought about it? Everything that you have accomplished in your life, started with that idea or dream that you first saw in your mind. You saw it, felt it and pursued it. You first saw what you wanted in your mind, by awakening your imagination. The feeling was so powerful that it moved your body to go towards it and attain it. Whether it was something small or something big, it all started with your mind.

Mom, it's time to dream again! It's time for you to focus on your true want and desire.

You see, you are that magic genie. You have the power to make any dream come true, no matter how impossible it may seem. You have done it before, you can do it again.

Mom, you need to wake up your imagination and bring to life what you want to see happen in your life. You need to be able to dream again. When you do you will begin to create the magic.

Start by seeing clearly in your mind exactly what you want. Now, this can't be very hard to do, because you know what it is just as much as I know. You want this more than anything in the world. Here, maybe I can help.

See in your mind your beautiful child, and they are happy and healthy. Picture them in your mind with a healthy body, laughing and sharing their life with you.

There is your child, smiling and looking you in the eye, and they are saying, "I love you, Mom."

Feel what it feels like to see your child happy and healthy. Feel it! Bring this image up in your mind and enjoy the feeling that envelopes your body as you dream. There it is, your perfect world.

Was I close, Mom? Is this your dream?

You can escape everything the world is showing you and what your child is presenting to you. You can escape. You can refuse to see it and believe it. You just need to go into your dreams, into your thoughts, into your imagination.

Go there, Mom. Go there often. Bring it up, bring it up in your mind every single moment of every single day. Dream, dream big. Dream so hard that you can feel it.

Feel your body begin to relax as you go to that dreamland where you and your child are living a wonderful life. You can have your perfect world, you just need to dream. Go there, Mom, go now!

And as you dream, feel yourself smiling. Feel the happiness that is radiating from you, from every cell of your body. Your body is reacting to the positive thought and it is sending that feeling outwards.

This is what burning brightly feels like. You can sense the warmth and so will those around you. Burn bright, Mom.

Glow so bright that others will want to come near you and feel it as well. They will want to be a part of it. They will want to bask in your sunshine.

Dream, dear Mom. Dream.

It is the one thing that no one else can control. It's all yours. No one else can change the images that enter your mind. Only you. Make it perfect. Make it yours.

It all starts with you Mom. Learn how to dream again.

Dream big!

Chapter 4

I PRAY

Hey Mom!

Well, here is another day, with you looking out at the world wondering what the day will bring. It's you against the world.

Sometimes being a Mom can be so lonely, can't it? There are those days where you just wish you had someone that knew exactly what you were going through and how you felt. If only someone understood.

Sure, there are good days, but there are those bad days with the feeling of helplessness. You seem so powerless sometimes, don't you? Who and what can you possibly turn to for help and guidance that will help ease your pain?

I bet there are so many times where you have asked for help and you didn't get what you needed. Asking for help is one thing, getting it is another. Who can you turn to for help when all else fails?

We all know and believe that there is a higher power. Depending on who you are and how you were raised, chances are you have a belief system in place. Whatever that higher power is to you, whether it is your God, or the Universe, one thing is for certain. Prayer is the last resort to even those who do not believe in a higher power. Even an atheist is known to have prayed on their death bed.

Prayer is the resource that seems to make all things better.

Have you been praying, Mom? When all else has failed and you are alone and feeling so vulnerable and unable to feel anymore, is prayer your final resort?

Have you been praying for that miracle? Have you asked God, a God, any God for that matter, even the Universe, for help?

Dear, Mom. It's okay to ask for help, and who better to ask than that invisible source that seems to have more power than any of us. That hidden energy that seems to envelope you with hope when nothing else seems to give you any comfort.

All alone with your thoughts and your mind full of such negativity, you finally find that peaceful place in your home, in a room or just in your mind, and you allow yourself to briefly escape to that being that is waiting for your request. It is like handing over everything you are holding and saying, "Here, please take this burden from me and make it all better."

When all else fails it is comforting to know that you can be alone with your thoughts and have that backup, just in case.

Have you been praying, pleading for that miracle? In those moments of despair and lost hope, have you asked for help through prayer?

Prayer kind of eases your mind and body, doesn't it, knowing that you can release this burden from yourself, admitting defeat, and asking something more powerful to take control.

I know that sometimes the only thing to do to give you hope and some peace of mind is to pray.

Whatever the situation, prayer can calm you and give you that state of mind that when all else fails, this magic form of wishing can help. Go ahead and lighten your load from your mind, Mom.

Pray, Mom.

Pray for yourself and pray for your child. Pray for your family and pray for their happiness and health. Fill your mind with everything you want. See it in your mind so clearly and then ask for it.

Allow your higher power to come to you and give you the guidance and direction you need to have and feel. Hand over all of that worry and doubt and let the energies take it from you!

Pray for what you want! Pray for a strong, healthy and happy child. And when you pray, send out all of the energy from yourself, from your soul, and feel it leaving you and your body as it goes out and seeks the answers.

Feel that energy as it leaves your body, your positive request that you emit as a vibration from yourself, as you send it out into the ether and it begins to search for what you need. Your prayers will be answered, Mom. I promise. We don't know how or by whom just yet, but answers will come.

The Universe does attract back to you what you send out. Have faith. Be patient and know that you and your child, if nothing else at all, you have that hidden force on your side out there doing some work, even if you cannot see it. You have at least put it out there. You did not sit still and do nothing. You sent out a message, an alert, an S.O.S.

Help is help. Where and how it comes doesn't matter. Just know that you have done your part.

You will get help, Mom. You are strong and you have a big heart. You want good for others in your life and you want happiness for yourself as well. You and your family all deserve to be happy and healthy, together.

Wish Mom, wish long and hard. That is prayer!

Imagine your true want, the true joy, the true happiness in your mind. Be thankful that it is now on its way. See it as if it is already here. Expect it. Have faith in it that your prayers are answered. No doubting it. No questioning it. No wondering if you are worthy. Just know that you deserve it and it is coming. Let the outer force find some answers for you. You may be surprised with what it sends back.

All you have to do is place the order and pray for it.

See in your mind what no one else can see. See the vision of your child, the child you remember being happy, with no cares or concerns. The child laughing and looking at you with those loving eyes. See your child in your mind as a successful, happy person. See your child vibrant, healthy and thriving. They are perfect. They are perfect in your mind.

See that!! Pray for that!!

Send out all of that positive energy and focus only on what you want to see in the future. Send that feeling, that love energy to your child. Engulf them with the love from your prayer.

Surround your child with the positive prayer of them being healthy, happy and healed. Pray and pray hard for that image. See it in your mind, and feel it like it is here. Ask for it with all of your heart!

And then have faith.

Know that it is coming.

Prayer opens your mind and allows the positive things in your mind to reach out and search for more positivity. It will seek out what you need and what you need will latch on to your frequency and it will be sent back to you. You will attract back exactly what you need.

This is why it is so important to ask for exactly what you want. Your image must be so clear. This powerful, positive image and feeling that you have for you and your family is so strong that only things that resonate with this feeling will be sent to you. All you have to do is be alert and ready to receive it when it comes.

Have faith. Have the expectation that you will receive.

Know that your prayer will be answered! It is coming. Expect it! Know it! Trust in yourself and your prayer!!

Prayers are answered every day. There are miracles every day!

Pray for your miracle!

Chapter 5

I AM GROWTH

Hey, Mom.

When is the last time you stopped to smell the roses? I know, I know, that is an old saying, but in so many ways it is a great saying.

It is to remind us to stop just for a brief moment and look at the beauty that surrounds us, the amazing world we live in and what it is capable of producing.

Roses really can be spectacular. Do you ever see them in the stores or in a neighbor's garden? You really do just want to stop and smell them, don't you? And for a brief moment your senses are taken away to a magical place with their beauty and fragrance.

Someone has taken the time to plant, cultivate, nurture and grow these beautiful specimens to perfection. They have also kept away all things negative and toxic that could harm their beautiful plants. It took just as much time and energy to weed and protect the plant from danger as it did to keep it strong and healthy. Sure, there were times where they didn't have the time or energy to fight the elements, but they knew that just one slip on their part could cost the health and safety of their treasured plant.

As long as the plant is cared for, nurtured and fed, it will continue to come back over and over again, bigger and stronger.

Nature is so predictable. If you really take a look around you now you can see a pattern happening. All things around you are either in a state of growth or in a state of disintegration.

We too are part of nature. We are all either growing or disintegrating. The goal is to stay in a constant state of growth. The minute you stop growing, there is only one other way, and that is disintegration.

Think about you, Mom, and the things you have taken the time to grow and nurture. I bet I can come up with a long list of things you have done in your life to help things grow.

Just like the roses, you have those things in your life that needed to be tended to, fed, nurtured and given a lot of your time and focus to ensure that they grew healthy and strong and beautiful.

You yourself are part of nature. You are always in a growth state. You are always taking care of yourself to ensure that you are tended to, cared for, fed and nurtured, so that you will continue to grow and be healthy and strong. Just like the roses, you need to be taken care of to ensure your constant growth.

Are you caring for yourself, Mom? Are you making sure that you are getting the nutrients, the sleep, the attention and the focus that your mind and body need to keep you growing?

Remember, Mom, you are either growing or disintegrating. You are part of nature.

There is a rule in nature, in the Universe, and in life. That which you focus on grows. Are you focusing on yourself and your growth?

Stop and think, Mom. Ask yourself this question all day long. Stop and look at what you are doing, what you are saying, what you are thinking. Ask yourself, "Am I focusing on my growth?"

Is what you are doing, what you are saying, what you are thinking, causing you to disintegrate? Is what you are doing, saying or thinking not feeding and nurturing your growth, but in fact, contributing to your disintegration?

When you are clear on your own growth, when you are positive that you are now in a constant state of growth, and you can feel it and you can see it, you are more able to help others to grow. You will have the energy and the desire to take on something else and help it in its growth. What will that be, Mom?

Mom, you must always be growing. You must always be growing, because when you are in growth, everything around you grows with you. You spread your nutrients to those that are close to you.

So, what does growth look and feel like?

Did you ever want to try something new, and you were excited but at the same time you were a little bit scared? You know that feeling where you have butterflies but you are having so much fun you are bursting inside? Well, that pretty much explains the feeling of growth. It is a positive happy feeling. It is knowing that you want something, you start to do it, and you are having such a great time doing it, you may even lose all track of time. That is growing!

It is a sense of purpose. It is reaching for a goal, a vision. You are moving towards a want, a desire. It is positive.

So, what does disintegration look and feel like?

Did you ever feel depressed, not having the energy or desire to even get out of bed? Do you spend your days spinning your wheels, doing the same things day in and day out with no excitement or reward? Well, that pretty much explains the feeling of disintegration. It is a negative feeling. It is not knowing what you want, wasting time and energy on unproductive things, and never caring about what you feed your mind or your body.

So, which one will it be, Mom?

Grow, Mom! Always be reaching for more. You need to use your mind more to start creating, to growing yourself, your hobbies, your desires. Focus on your health, your ideas, your self-esteem. Just grow you!

Try new things, introduce new ideas. Keep yourself in a positive state of growth. Grow yourself all day long. Nurture You! Deteriorating is not an option!

When you are healthy, positive and strong it spreads to everything in close proximity of you. That includes your child. Your energy will be felt by everyone around you.

Oh, dear, Mom, you have spent a huge part of your life caring and nurturing your child. You are a loving and giving person. You fed them, nurtured them, tended to them, year after year, and all you could envision was their wonderful growth and accomplishments in life. Just like the roses, you enjoyed their bloom as they grew year after year.

And just like that, your beautiful flower has been exposed to something so toxic, that it is making it impossible for it to grow, but instead is forcing their disintegration. And there you are powerless, trying to save your rose, hoping and praying that the toxin will stop and you can go back to tending and growing your flower.

Mom, you are there to help with their growth, and only their growth. That's what Moms do. You help them grow their mind, their body, their health and their lives.

But things have been a little fuzzy lately. You have not been clear on how to help yourself stay in growth, could you possibly be unclear on how to help your child stay in growth?

The last thing a mom would do is contribute to their disintegration, right? How does one know the difference? Are you helping your child grow or disintegrate? Ask yourself, Mom. Ask yourself this all day long.

Stop and look at what you are doing, what you are saying, what you are thinking. "Am I focusing on my child's growth?"

Or is what you are doing, what you are saying, what you are thinking, helping them to disintegrate? Is what you are doing, saying or thinking not feeding and nurturing their growth, but in fact, contributing to their disintegration.

Pay attention, Mom!

You need to clearly see when you are nurturing and feeding their growth. You need to clearly see when you are contributing and helping their disintegration. Can you tell the difference?

There is only one choice for you and your child. That is the path of growth. You will always be focusing on your child's growth, and never be participating in their disintegration of their mind or their body.

You will let them know that you love them so much, that you care for them so much that you will do anything and everything you can for their growth. You will be there for them for anything they need for their growth, to become healthy happy human beings. Mom is always there to help.

You will nurture them with positive reinforcement, love and reassurance, and you will feed their body and their minds.

You will let them know that you love them so much, that you care for them so much that you cannot be a part of their disintegration. You cannot support them harming, hurting and poisoning something you love so much. It is too painful for you to watch. Mom will not take part in helping them with anything that will harm them, especially their toxins.

You will not contribute in any way that is negative, hateful or toxic to their body or their mind.

You are Mom. The caretaker of this beautiful specimen that is your child.

There is a fine line between your child and your child's addiction. Tend to and care for your child. Nurture their body and mind positively.

Eventually, your child will know and understand that as long as they are on the right path, the path for growth, Mom is there right by their side.

They will know that they can rely on you to be there for their journey as long as it is for their benefit. They will know that you love them and will do only the best for them to grow. As long as they choose to grow, Mom will do whatever it takes to help.

You will become the one constant in their life that they know they can turn to for positive reinforcement and help when they need it as long as they are the path to growth. There is no room for disintegration. Not on Mom's watch!

You deserve a happy and healthy life and you are doing whatever it takes to have that life. Your child deserves a happy and healthy life. Let them see what that looks like.

Chapter 6

I AM RESPECTED

Hey, Mom.

I see you. I know who you are. I know you are there. So kind. So sweet. So caring.

I know you well because you are Mom. Ever caring and loving who only wants the best for their child. I know. I know!

Imagine being a child that is so loved by you. Imagine how that love must feel. No one in the world will ever have that kind of love. No married couple, no siblings, no other mother and child. Your love for your child is the strongest force you have ever felt in your life. And you are the only one that knows how that feels. You are Mom!

You do know deep down that your child loves you the same way? You do know that, right?

Even though it doesn't feel like it right now, you and your child have a bond that will be there until the end. Your child loves you so much. You know they do. Sometimes you may not feel it or see it, but it is there.

Remember when they were small and you were the most important thing to them? It was you. It was. Remember that, Mom. As they grew they found other interests, other friends, other loves, but they knew you were always there, even if just in the shadows, you were always there should they ever feel unloved, uncared for, or unappreciated. They knew that you had their back no matter what!

Mom's there always! They know where to find you.

You are this amazing person, who is so giving and loving, you too deserve to be loved. You too deserve to be treated with the love and respect that you gave your family all of those years.

Treat others how you want to be treated. It is that simple. It doesn't matter who it is or in what situation, you always treat others how you want to be treated, don't you, Mom?

You are so worthy of love and respect. You are a warm and caring person full of love. You are loveable and you need to feel loved. You were raised with it and you continue to give it to others. You deserve to be treated with that same love and respect.

You know this so well, and you have so much self-respect for yourself too, don't you, Mom? How are you going through life right now, Mom? Are you being treated with respect?

People tend to treat one another based on what one allows. Are people speaking to you respectfully the way you speak to them? Are people treating you with respect the way you treat them?

When you come face to face with a person who doesn't respect you or treat you kindly, you can feel that negativity can't you, Mom? Can't you?

You are a beacon of love and respect, so when hatred and disrespect come your way you can feel it. You can sense it. It affects you! You are repelled by it, especially because you would never treat someone else that way.

It goes so against who you are and what you believe, and what you stand for. It shakes your entire core being. How could someone be so rude and aggressive? Shocking!!

How could anyone talk to you that way, Mom? Someone so full of love and kindness as yourself. Someone who knows and understands their self-worth, and has self-respect. You don't allow yourself to be treated in such a manner, not by anyone!

Right, Mom? Anyone!!

It doesn't matter how that negativity comes your way. Whether it is from a stranger, a co-worker, a family member, or your child.

The line in the sand can sometimes get skewed when we are dealing with our child. That sweet child that you raised with love and respect, and that always treated you with love and respect, would never do anything to hurt you, would they?

How's your self-respect today, Mom? How is your confidence level and your self-worth?

It's one thing to be beaten down by a stranger, but when it is your child, you can sometimes feel defeated and worthless. It's easy to feel helpless and out of control. How can someone disrespect their own Mom?

Remember this, Mom. A person is not capable of loving and respecting another individual if they are not able to love and respect themselves first.

Someone from the outside seeing you full of self-respect, who cannot see it for themselves, will definitely not want to see it in you. They don't believe it can exist. It is foreign to them and it doesn't feel good. It is a positive trait that is repelling their negativity. It literally hurts them to see it.

A person that is insecure, with no self-worth and no self-respect, they cannot relate to having what you have. They don't believe it to be true. They hate themselves so much they will resent you being able to have so much love and respect for yourself.

They are not capable of giving love and respect because they are not capable of receiving love and respect. That is because in their mind, they are not deserving of it.

If they could just make it go away, they won't have to deal with it. They won't have to step up and learn that love and self-respect for themselves and others is a possibility. They are so weak and out of control, the easiest thing for them is to not step up and love themselves, but to have you come down to their level.

It is too hard, uncomfortable and exhausting to step up and fight for themselves and their self-worth. It's easier to just lay in denial and be controlled by their darkness.

If they can cause you to fall and lose the self-respect and self-worth you have for yourself, it is proof to them that it doesn't exist. It will justify to them that they will never have it themselves.

Why learn how to be in the light, when I can just make the light go away? For they are the ones in the darkness. They are the ones that are struggling with their own self-worth. They do not love and respect themselves, so how can they possibly love and respect others. That includes you.

But they don't know who they are dealing with, do they? You are Mom, your child is in a dark place, but you don't do dark, remember? You are the light.

You are so strong and confident that when a person is persistent in trying to bring you down to their level, the harder they try to bring you down and to have you react, the stronger you become.

You do not accept disrespect and hatred. You are a positive being and you repel the negative, do you not? Just like the negative person may repel and reject your positivity. You are a positive person that repels and rejects negativity.

And the louder that one gets against you, the stronger one gets against you, throwing their stones to try and tear you down, to make you stop because they are feeling the discomfort of love, the firmer you plant yourself in the ground.

You are so aware and able to see that the anger is coming from fear. Remember, you come from caring and loving. The more abusive the words, the more you can see their self-hatred and their despair. They are scared about who they are and their situation. So dark. So, so dark. But you continue to be positive, shining the light, so bright, so, so bright!

And when you are in a situation where a person does not treat you the way you deserve to be treated, you are Mom, and you are in charge. You are the one setting the standard.

Your presence in a room is a privilege not a right. Others must learn, that for you to allow them to be around you, they need to see you and treat you a certain way. They need to deserve to be in your company.

It is sometimes very hard to stay positive and shining brightly when there is someone or something constantly trying to turn you dark. Especially, when it is your own child.

Your light is imposing on their darkness. The more they throw their stones at your stature, the stronger you become. You can take it. You don't crumble and fall. You continue to stand your ground and respect yourself, love yourself, and you continue to lead, and show what self-respect and self-love looks like.

It takes a lot of energy but you are up for the challenge.

Stay strong, Mom! Step out with confidence and self-assurance. Be that lighthouse ever so strong and glowing in the distance, always there to help guide.

Respectful. Deserving of respect. Respected.

Stand brightly before people that need to see and feel the warmth and brightness of your glow.

If someone does not want to be in your light because the glare from your brightness hurts their eyes, then they can learn to adjust. They must learn to be in your presence. They must adapt to bask in the light and heat of your love.

You will never lower yourself to someone else's level. They must learn to step up to yours! You are the example.

Show people that when you are faced with something that is trying to control you, something that is trying to break you and take over you as a person, as a human being, that you have the strength to overcome it and win the battle.

Be the example that shows your child how to stand up for yourself, your dreams, and your life. Show them what that looks like.

When you demonstrate the respect you have for yourself, by taking care of yourself, and living a life of purpose, you are showing that you love yourself and want to continue and grow to share yourself with others. You are proof that it is possible to have a happy and successful life.

With every one of your successes is the proof that it can be done. No matter the size of the goal or dream, you are the example that it is possible to achieve, that there is success, no matter how large or small.

And you will celebrate your successes with everyone because with each success, there is a glimmer of hope for others that they too can be successful and achieve….no matter what the goal. Show them how it is done.

Show them how when you have hope, and love and self-respect for yourself anything is possible. Help others see new ideas and dreams for themselves. After all, if you can do it, so can they.

Be the example for others that no matter how hard, how impossible, and how dark the situation, if you just love yourself enough, and have enough self-respect in yourself, you can overcome any challenge.

You are the proof, Mom! Prove it! For others are watching and learning from you.

Remember Mom, you are the guide.

You are Mom. You are the beacon of hope. You stand firm, and you stand tall. You know how to love and you know how to be loved. You deserve to be treated with love.

You have self-respect and you respect others. You deserve to be respected. You have self-worth and you love yourself. You are the light.

Allow others to step into your light.

Teach others how to shine brightly. Teach them. Teach them to fight. Teach them that they are worth it! Teach them about the light.

Chapter 7

I ACCEPT

Life is funny isn't it, Mom?

Here we are, all of us humans, living the same point in life on this timeline together. We all started differently and we will all end differently, but in reality, we are all just a group of people going through life together at this same moment in time.

Everyone else is just in our history or in our future. We are the only ones in the world all here at the same time. We are all experiencing different things, at different hours, and different places. We are all doing what it takes to survive in our own little part of Earth.

For the most part, we have no road map, no secret path to lead and guide us. We are all just making it up as we go along, doing what we need to do to survive.

We all have different personalities, different experiences, and different situations. No two of us are going along the same journey in life exactly the same. We are all so individual. No one can know or feel what we are going through, as it is our own unique journey.

Amazing isn't it? All of the millions of people in this world, going through their day to day lives, doing what it takes to survive.

Imagine what others are going through? What successes, what losses, what catastrophes and what miracles are others experiencing right now?

Can you imagine? Everyone is fighting their own battle in their own back yard. Oh sure, we may get a glimpse into someone else's life now and again and even share in their experience, but for the most part we are all going it alone in our little bubble.

It would seem sort of odd wouldn't it, for you to judge another person and how they are dealing with their life, wouldn't it?

Can you imagine judging a stranger and how they are going through life? How could you do it? You would need to know exactly what their situation is, how they grew up, their personality, and their beliefs.

It doesn't make sense does it? Judging others and why and how they do things is so subjective and frankly, so personal.

And what is judgement anyways, Mom? Is it imposing what we currently believe and think and then compare it to the actions of others? Are we pigeon holing people and asking them to fit in our pre-conceived form of how things should be done based on our own opinions?

Can we really expect people to fit in to something our way or else come to the assumption that there is something wrong with them?

Funny how people think they know how things should be and how others should be doing it. But, how can we escape it? We have been judged most of our lives. Think about it. We have always been judged right from childhood. How we do in school, how we act, what we wear, what we say.

Judgment is all around us. But when you really look at it more closely, most of the judgement we have is quite useless, don't you think? What do we care what someone else wears? There are people with no clothes on their backs. Yet, we judge people by a label on their shirts. We are judged by the car we drive, the jobs we have, our partners. Why? What purpose does it serve? And who has the final judgment call?

Who are we to judge anyway? We are all individuals with our own path in this life. We are all facing different obstacles and we are all dealing with them the best we can.

Are you feeling judged? Do you walk with confidence knowing that you are accepted or do you fear that you are being judged somehow?

It's hard being judged by others isn't it, Mom? They don't know you or your life, or your experiences.

How can anyone judge you, your family, or your situation, without even knowing your life and how you got here? How dare anyone judge, right? It makes no sense.

But there is one judgment that super cedes all others. The worse judgment of all. The harshest and most harmful and hurtful judgment. This is the judgment we make on ourselves.

Do you find that you judge yourself, Mom? Have you been telling yourself some pretty awful things about who you are or how you have been doing things? Have you been critical of yourself?

I want to assure you right now that you are totally normal in doing it. We all do it. It is how we have been taught to think and act. We are judged, we judge. Unfortunately, the worse judgment we give is to ourselves.

Mom, all of this judgment, is it making you feel more defeated and a failure? How many hours a day do you spend telling yourself awful things about yourself? I hope you are not wasting your great mind on such things.

You are Mom. You don't have time for negativity. You know that this is a waste of time and that you need your energy for more productive things. If you are ready to release judgment there is only one thing you need to do.

Be accepting. That's it. Don't fight things, analyze things, and even worse judge things. Just start to accept things as they are. You know that you can't change the past and you cannot predict the future.

Why not then have a clear starting point in life. If you can accept a thing or a situation, you can now focus on moving past it. It's time to let go and move on. What can you stop judging today, Mom? What can you look at and finally just accept? Start by looking at yourself. Practice non-judgment on you, Mom.

No more judging you for what you did, how you did it, what others do, what you do. No more judging your looks, your voice, your weight or what you say or what you don't say.

Just accept things for what they are. You can accept that you are an imperfectly perfect human being going through life doing what it takes to survive.

When you take away judgment, it all seems so freeing suddenly, doesn't it?

Accepting yourself for the amazing individual that you are is your first step. You have never done life before, and you are learning as you go. There is no right or wrong, there just is what there is. Things happen, events happen, and results happen. Experiences just are!

You are going through life the same way everyone else is in this moment of time. Everything is done by trial and error. You are still here and you still have a lot of time left, so you must be doing something right!

Accept that you are doing a great job at life and that you are ready to move forward with more learning. Accept yourself for who you are right here and now.

When you finally accept how perfect of an individual you are, and free yourself from the negativity of judgment, you will begin to see and accept others around you.

You will focus more on accepting others for who they are and their situations. You will learn to let go of judgment and replace it with acceptance and understanding.

Accept that they too are imperfectly perfect human beings going through their lives doing what it takes to survive. When you accept more freely, you become more understanding and compassionate.

Accept yourself, Mom. No more judgment. Accept who you are and how you have lived your life. You can't change it so you might as well accept it.

Free yourself from self-judgment. No more comparisons. No more standards or bars that you have to reach. Accept yourself for who you are right now, right here, for who you are today. Be more confident as the future starts right here, right now!

As you become accustomed to not judging, but accepting, you will learn to not judge others but to accept them. People will feel it, and they will know and trust that they can be with you, and whatever mistakes they make in their life, you will not judge. You will become that safe space.

Those that are tired of being judged and feeling inferior will want to be in your presence, because they know you are so accepting of them. You will attract trust and respect because you are so accepting.

Eventually, those people will learn how to accept themselves and to stop being such harsh critics of themselves. And it will all be because of you, Mom!

What does acceptance look like, Mom, for you? Can you free yourself and others from judgment?

Accept yourself, Mom. Accept yourself for who you are and where you are right now. Accept your situations, Mom. You are a powerful and strong human being that has faced many things before. Look forward to the future.

Accept others, Mom. Accept them for who they are and where they are right now. Accept them and their journey in this life, and the part you are playing in it.

There is no manual to life. You just live it.

For you are Mom. Accept it!

Chapter 8

I AM LIFE

Hey Mom!

Do you ever just stop and think about how amazing you are? I don't just mean as a Mom. We all know that you are the amazing, wonderful individual that people can only dream about being one day.

I'm thinking about you as a human being. You are a living, breathing human! How amazing is life, really? When you look at how you were put together one cell at a time, pieced together until you were formed into this one-of-a-kind person. Isn't it amazing? Life is so precious.

But there is just one catch. This amazing human body can only function with the right nurturing. Without food and water, it will disintegrate and cease to exist. All you have to do is feed it what it needs and it will run the best it can until the day you die.

Your body needs to have the right input so that you can have the right output.

We really have no problem thinking about food and drink every day, do we? For many of us, it is the only thing on our minds. After all, who doesn't like to eat and drink? In fact, the majority of people are trying to curb the amount of food they consume. I think we can agree that nourishment for most of us is not the concern.

There is one thing that we all take for granted however, that is even more important than what we feed ourselves.

It is breathing. Without breathing, your body does not survive. Your breathing is the most important function your body does, and for the most part, it is the last thing you probably think about, isn't it? It is like you are on autopilot. But it is the most important part of your being.

Think about it, Mom. You took that first breath when you were born. That breath was the first sign that a new life has begun!

It is crucial. It is the life source that you rely on to keep your body functioning. Yet, it is probably something you are not even thinking about, is it, Mom?

When you really take a moment and think about it, are you breathing right now? I know you are because you are alive, but have you ever stopped and paid attention to your breathing? Now that I mention it, did you just take a deep breath in? Funny how the most important thing in your life is the last thing on your mind.

You seem to be breathing without any thought. Your body is running right now, and breathing on its own, without any input from you.

But even though you are breathing, for some reason, I bet you feel like you are out of air right now, am I right, Mom? Almost like the life has literally been sucked out of you. You are only doing the bare minimum of what you need to do to keep alive. You probably feel like you have had the wind knocked out of you completely.

Remember as a child, holding your breath under water until you couldn't do it any longer and you burst out of the water and let out a gasp for air? Sometimes it feels like you are holding your breath right now, doesn't it, Mom? Just breathing takes all the energy you have.

Maybe you have been alternating between the shallow breathing that accompanies worry and despair and the hyperventilating that comes with anxiety. What does normal breathing even feel like anymore?

Can you imagine yourself just breathing a normal, healthy breath? No more holding your breath. No more gasping for air. Just nice and easy cleansing breaths that would feed your lungs, your body, and your mind.

When is the last time you really breathed Mom? Well, it's time you came up for air, Mom! How about you do it right now?

Take a nice, slow, deep breath right now. Nice and slow. And let it out nice and slow. Doesn't that feel nice? Did you notice for the first time in a long time your own breathing?

You don't really think about it much, do you?

Let's try that again. Take in a nice, slow, breath and think about that wonderful air that you are absorbing. Really focus on the air that you are allowing into your body. And then release it nice and slow.

Breathing is amazing, isn't it? Keep breathing, Mom! With each breath you take in, feel the energy that the oxygen is feeding your lungs, your body, and your mind. Nice and slow.

Why not take a moment now to free your mind of all thoughts and decide that you are just going to relax and enjoy your breathing?

Slowly blow out all of the air in your lungs through your mouth and when there is nothing left, close your mouth and allow your nose to slowly breathe in that new breath of fresh air. Feel it as it fills up your lungs with the force that is keeping you alive. Slowly push it out with your mouth as you prepare for your next breath.

With each breath that comes in, see yourself being replenished, renewed and injected with energy and life. With each breath that goes out, feel yourself relaxed and in control of your body and your mind. Enjoy this time as you allow yourself this cleansing of your mind and body.

You deserve this relaxation. You deserve this time. You deserve to just breathe.

Feel every cell of your body accepting the air as it moves in and through you. Feed yourself and your body with the air that is so nourishing. Feel yourself coming back to life.

Think about nothing else. Focus only on the air you are breathing. Can you do that for yourself right now, Mom? Can you focus only on you, on yourself, and your breathing?

Of course, you can!

Keep breathing, Mom. It is what you need to survive. Survive Mom! You are alive, and you are breathing. Always ensure that you are replenishing yourself with your life source.

With each breath bring in the freshness of life, and with each breath out, release the thoughts, the worries, the stress, the anxiety. Feel it all leave your body with each exhale.

Keep breathing Mom. With each breath feel yourself coming more and more back to life. Fill yourself with what you need to survive. Breathe, Mom. Breathe, Mom.

Breathe that sigh of relief as you feel yourself come alive.

Mom, you are such an amazing part of this vast world. Your whole being revolves around you breathing. Enjoy the air that is around you. Fill those lungs with healthy, nurturing air.

Go for walks, climb hills and mountains, and allow yourself to take in the fresh air that you and your body have been craving.

Fill yourself and your lungs.

When you finally learn to breathe again, Mom, and you feel yourself replenished and alive again, you will have the energy and strength to help others who are suffocating to come up for air.

You are the holder of the oxygen mask. You must first take a breath from it, so that you have the strength to pass it to the person who needs it next.

It all starts with your breath.

Chapter 9

I AM IN CONTROL

Hey, Mom?

Another day in the life of a Mom, right? You wake up, think about the day and what might come your way, and then you decide how you are going to face it.

Sometimes things seem quiet and ordinary and other days they seem crazy and turbulent. But either way, you have to get out of bed and face it, don't you? That is because you as Mom are always on! You never have a day off. Mom is a constant entity and is always there for everyone.

How are you coping with all of that, Mom?

Coping seems like such an ordinary word, but when you really think, it is packed with so many definitions. In a nutshell, coping is what you do each day just for you to get by. It is the bare minimum of what you need to help you move through your day.

How are coping now, Mom?

Is it that cup of coffee that gets your engine running, your phone calls to friends for support, or is there something more?

You are human, Mom, and there is only so much a person can take. No one is invincible. But if what you are doing to cope is causing you to go down or disintegrate, then you may need to take a closer look.

Let's start with your past. How did your family cope when there was disruption in the home? Where did you learn how to cope?

Did you learn healthy coping skills or destructive actions?

Think about it. Think about it very closely, because chances are, you are coping the same way you learned from your upbringing. Have you been taught how to handle things in a crisis? Are you coping in a healthy way?

For many people, their coping skills are very limited. Their first order of business when something bad comes their way is avoidance. Avoiding the problem or issue makes it go away. Not very logical, but it is a quick cure to a problem.

Even worse however, is to remove any feelings or connection to the issue, especially when it is one that is very emotional.

Self-medication in some form or another is a quick fix to not have to feel the stress and anxiety related to the event. The pain of something is so bad, you will do anything to numb it. This is a quick and easy way to just not have to deal with something. Not very effective in solving anything, but it ends the situation if anywhere, in your mind.

How we cope with situations is purely relative. How do you cope, Mom?

Are you hiding away from the world, maybe reflecting on the past, always looking in that rear view mirror, full of regret, dwelling on things that can't be changed? It's hard to be alone with such negative thoughts. This type of action can easily take you deep into a depression and into a very dark place. Mom doesn't do dark, right?

If you are hiding away Mom, it is understandable. It is safer there. Avoiding the present and what may lie ahead is sometimes necessary, but not the best avenue. Remember, you are Mom, and you are up for the challenge. You face your obstacles. No dwelling, just accepting. If you are hiding away and avoiding, take a step out and start facing your reality and prepare yourself to move on.

Hey, Mom, how about blaming others or even worse, yourself for everything that has happened in your life so far? Is this how you cope? Do you focus on finding who to pin this on? Sometimes explaining things in a way that it was your or someone else's fault justifies the event somehow. Dangerous waters as you may have to carry guilt or the role of victim for the rest of your life.

Not the characteristic of you, Mom. Right?

When things happen and you spiral, do you call your friends or family to complain and download on them? Is this how you have learned to cope? Releasing all of your negative energy on others, allowing them to share in your pain. Sometimes this can be instant relief, having that shoulder to cry on can be therapeutic. But if this becomes your go-to day in and day out, will people look forward to hearing from you? Doesn't sound like Mom behavior to me. You are the go-to person, right?

Are you finding ways to just turn off your mind, to be swept away into another fantasy world where you don't have to think or see anything on your own. Maybe you binge watch tv or play video games or gamble.

Sounds a bit destructive doesn't it? Are these any of the ways you are coping, Mom?

Whatever way you find to cope, Mom, is it in a healthy way? Coping is a learned behavior. It is a reaction to an action. It is a mechanism to help you deal with an issue at hand.

How are you dealing with things? Mom, you are facing some of the biggest, most emotional obstacles of your life. How are you coping with it all?

First of all, it doesn't matter how you got here or what is happening in your life. What matters is how you face it and deal with it. The past is done, it's over, and you cannot change it. It's time to stand tall and face your challenges in a healthy manner.

Just being aware of how you are coping is the first step. How do you react when faced with a challenge, any challenge?

Do you isolate? Do you implode, explode? This is your survival mechanism. You need to protect yourself, your feelings and your mind to survive. Reacting is one thing, accepting the way you react as part of your normal behavior going forward is not.

You want to learn to cope in a way that is healthy and productive. This takes time and energy, but you are Mom! You are a strong person and a leader. A guide. You are always calm, caring and wise.

How you cope with your day to day is your choice. It should soothe you and help you deal with the task, the pain, or the event at hand. Sometimes it is the only thing you have to keep you going.

I want you to now notice if you are still coping or if you have now accepted your coping mechanism as a behavior. Has it now become a part of you and if so, it is serving you? Are you still escaping somehow?

It's time to step back and take a close look at you, Mom. You've been focusing on everyone else for so long, maybe it is you that needs the attention for a change.

Remember, your actions affect those around you. If you are in a negative state, you will be surrounding those around you with that negativity as well. You are Mom. You are positive, after all, you are the light!

You handle things with care and logic. You are confident and strong.

You have a lot going on, Mom, and you are so good at being Mom, you know what is best for you moving forward.

Mom, take care of yourself. How you cope can be positive or negative. Find the coping mechanism that keeps you positive and growing. You know what that looks like and feels like.

And remember, however way you learn how to cope, those around you are watching and learning as well.

Mom, you know what you need to do.

"Never allow someone to be your priority

while allowing yourself to be their option."

Mark Twain

Chapter 10

I AM FREE

Hi Mom!

Don't you love being a Mom? There is nothing like the joy and happiness of raising a child, is there?

Oh, sure there were days where you just wanted to lock yourself in your room and avoid them completely, but for the most part, you enjoyed seeing your child most when they were happy and free and just enjoying being a kid.

It was always so fun to see the look on that face when you bought them something new, maybe a new toy, or some candy, and they would be so thankful. "Thanks, Mom," they would exclaim. Maybe it was even followed by an approving hug. Oh, that feeling of successfully pleasing your child. There is nothing like seeing them so happy.

You did good, Mom. You made your child happy and their happiness spilled over to you. Whether it was a full-blown birthday party, or just a day playing at home with their friends, that smile on their face melted you and made you feel great.

It's interesting how one small person can give you so much pleasure. From that little being you were capable of measuring your happiness. When your child wasn't happy or was displeased about something or someone in their life, you felt it too, didn't you, Mom?

When they came home from school and had an issue with a friend, or a teacher, and they shared their anger or frustration, you were there to listen and you felt their frustration right along with them. You were there for them, Mom, weren't you? Their fear and anger spilled over to you and you were not happy until they were happy again.

And you know as a Mom you jumped into gear and you set out to make your child happy. You would console them, help them see what they needed to do, even guided them with the right choices. Your goal was for them to be happy again. Because after all, you are unhappy until they are happy.

You were there with them every step of the way until things were resolved and you could share in that happiness again. You would do anything to see that smile again. What you would give just to see them smile again.

But you of course knew there were times where you knew best, right, Mom? You weren't always the good guy in their minds. There were times that were challenging and you had to risk the disapproving glare from your child.

When they would ask for things that you knew were not good for them and you had to say, "No." Maybe it was that candy before dinner, or a sleep over at a friend's house. Even though you knew it was what they wanted you had to put your foot down and say, "No."

You made so many choices that you felt were in the best interest for your child. That wasn't easy, was it, Mom? Your child was angry with you for not giving them what they wanted. It seemed like the end of the world to them when you wouldn't let them have what they wanted, and it felt really bad. That anger and resentment was directed right at you. That didn't feel good, did it?

But you are Mom. You know what is best for your child and you knew how to separate the good from the bad for your child. Deep down you knew that this was just an event and that it would pass. You knew that the bond between the two of you was stronger than the thing or place that your child wanted at that moment. You would survive and move on.

You were confident taking charge, knowing you were right, protecting your child and making the decision to keep them from something that you felt was not in their best interest. And most of the time you won.

It didn't matter how long they nagged you, the tantrums, the slamming of the doors, you stood your ground because you knew they had to listen to you. But things have kind of changed now haven't they, Mom?

Suddenly, the thing that is bad for your child, that can destroy your child, is something out of your control. And their pain and frustration are starting to cross over to you, aren't they, Mom?

You can see and feel everything that is happening because they aren't happy any more. And if they aren't happy, Mom isn't happy. Oh, what you would do to see that pain and frustration in their face go away, even for a brief moment, so that you can once again see them happy.

Really, Mom? What would you do?

What they now want, is something they desperately want. Nothing has changed. The begging and the pleading may come in a different form, a different way, but it is there.

They are full of fear and frustration and you are feeling it. But you as Mom are always there to stand firm and say, "No," to what is not in their best interest.

Are you still that strong, firm Mom? Are you saying "No?"

It's hard to say, "No," when you are desperately seeking that smile from your child, even for a brief moment. Are you willing to say, "Yes" to something just to feel that warm smile and approval again? Are you, Mom?

Are you doing anything that would ease your child's pain even for a fleeting moment, just in order for you not to feel that pain anymore? When you see that spark in their eyes, that dimple in their cheek. Could you still say, "No," to that sweet face?

It was hard to say, "No," to your child then and it is hard to say it to your child now. After all, the resentment and anger are louder and stronger.

But in the end, you are Mom, and you will not take part in something that is not good for your child. Never. You are Mom.

You are the provider and nurturer to help your child grow and lead a healthy successful life. You would never take part in anything that would help in the disintegration and harmfulness to your child.

Unless of course, you are relying on your child's happiness to dictate your happiness.

Are you craving the feelings you would receive when your child displayed happiness and acceptance of you and your gifts? Are you, Mom? Are you relying on your child to make you happy?

Are you addicted to your child's happiness? Of course, you are. You lived through your child for so many years. How can you possibly stop now? You are now living the nightmare with them, and you want to just wake up and be normal again. If only they were happy, then you could be happy. Is that how it works, Mom?

But isn't putting the onus on someone else to make you happy quite a tall order? How could anyone have such a responsibility to make another person happy? Are you relying on your child to make you happy?

How about you take that away for now? How about you let go of that for now?

How do you think your child would feel if you took away that burden from them? What if they weren't responsible for your happiness anymore? Do you think that would take a load off of their shoulders?

It's time for a punch in the stomach, Mom. Your child is not responsible for you and your happiness. Your child does not owe you anything. They are not responsible for how you feel, how you act, how you are, how you think. They are responsible for none of it.

I'm sorry, Mom, but your happiness is all on you. You are responsible for your own happiness. You are the only one that can make you happy.

And I know that a mother is only as happy as her unhappiest child. So, I get it. But it's time to let go, Mom.

I want you to think about this very carefully. I want you to be very clear on what I am about to say here.

Your child is what makes you happy. Not their happiness. If you rely on their happiness for you to be happy, you are putting a very heavy weight on their shoulders.

Your child is unhappy about their addiction, and so are you. It goes without saying. But you need to separate your child from the addiction. You can still be happy and you can still bring happiness to your child. You need to first see your child.

What makes you happy is caring and nurturing your child. Continue to do that. Give them what they need to clear their minds of the darkness. Give them space, encouragement, positive ideas and thoughts. Nourish, tend to them, take care of them. Be happy knowing that you are feeding them with healthy thoughts and motivation.

Keep them free from judgments, negative ideas, or thoughts. Only fill their minds with compassion, support, and encouragement. Show your child your happiness in them. Don't always be expecting it from them, dear, Mom.

Letting go, does not mean letting go of the love of your child. Letting go means freeing yourself from the need of them providing your happiness.

You still have a child that brings you happiness. You have been focusing on the wrong thing, the addiction. It is the addiction that is making you and your child unhappy. Not your child. It's not your child that is causing all of this unhappiness. It is the addiction.

You may not love your child's habits and you may not love their choices in life. But you will always love them. The person. The child. Your child.

Love the child, hate the habit. Feed the child, starve the habit

Your child is still capable of making you happy. Look for the happiness in them. Help them see what makes them happy. Look for it in your child because it is there. You just need to look in the right places.

Keep loving, Mom. Keep guiding.

Remember, you are MOM!

Chapter 11

I AM HERE

Hey, Mom!

How are you doing today? Some days, doesn't it seem so hard just to put one foot in front of the other?

Every day seems to roll into the next with no changes, the same things over and over again. The same thoughts, the same feelings. Each day sometimes just resembles and is a repeat of yesterday. If only things could be different.

But you continue on. You wake up and you do your usual things hoping that today will be the day that something will change. Anything. Just a glimmer of hope that the life you are currently living will all be a bad dream and that you will wake up and look forward to the day.

If only there was a magic wand to make everything wonderful again. Or better yet, someone or something to help you feel better every morning so that you could at least feel a sense of normalcy and to have a shot of energy or motivation to get you through the day. Wouldn't it be great if you had someone close by to share your feelings with and comfort you when you need it most?

Sometimes you feel so alone don't you? If only you had someone that knew exactly how you felt and that you felt comfortable with enough to share your deepest, darkest secrets and emotions.

Well what if I told you that you are not alone. In fact, there is someone that you haven't seen in a while, and she is really in need, and she is waiting for you to check in and pay her some attention.

I know you know her. In fact, you pass her every day and frankly, I don't mean to be direct, but you tend to ignore her. That's not like you. The warm caring Mom that is there for everyone. That's definitely not like you to ignore someone who needs your attention.

You've seen her. I know you have. It's usually when you are getting out of the shower or bath. You've seen her in that steamy mirror and you have shot her that quick non- assuming glance.

Oh, I know that sometimes you stop and you give her a moment of your attention. But it is probably just to make a judgment about her skin, or her weight, maybe even her hair. You've thought about stopping and spending some time with her, but yet being in your state of mind, it is taking every ounce of energy just to get showered and dressed, who has the time to stop and chat.

Most days you ignore her completely, not even noticing she is there. But what do you expect? Your mind is so clouded with the thoughts of the day ahead and what turmoil or angst awaits you who has the time to stop and check in. Just the thought of not focusing on your despair for one moment seems exhausting, doesn't it?

What if just for today, you stopped that negative chatter going on in your mind.

Just for today, why not stop and do things a little differently. Rather than operating in the same manner of every other day where you mindlessly go through your actions, you order yourself to do something different. What if rather than thinking about things you have no control over, you decide to step up and think about something you can control.

How about it, Mom? Are you up for the challenge? Of course, you are. You are Mom and you can do anything.

Let's slow things down.

The next time you are in that bathroom, and you are walking past that mirror, and you glance over and see her reflection looking straight at you, how about you stop and take a closer look.

What if you finally stop and pay some attention to that person that you have been ignoring.

You know what I think? I think she needs you right now. Not later, not tomorrow…..right now! Go see her right now. You need to, Mom. You are so giving and caring. Go to her now.

Look at her very closely. She is the one looking a little forlorn. A little scared, maybe even a little lost. There's something about her though isn't there? Even though she has this timid almost helpless feel to her, you can see that deep down she has this magnetism and appeal about her that you just want to get behind and support.

There is something about her, Mom. It's like she is wanting out but doesn't know what to do. You have to help her!

In fact, you are the only person that can help her right now. You are the only one that can see her and can connect with her. You can't ignore her any longer. You have to do something, Mom!

If you don't, no one will. Stop everything, Mom, and finally take a look, a real look, at the reflection before you.

It's time to slow things down and rather than rushing by that amazing individual you stop and take a moment and really focus on her.

Who is that person that stands before you?

Stop and really take a close look at her. She seems all alone and in need of some attention. Is she okay?

Look closely at that warm human being with those loving eyes that are gazing back at you. The eyes of a Mom that is suffering and in despair, and that wants so much to fix everything and make everything better, but doesn't know how.

How can you help that person lost inside those beautiful eyes? Really gaze at her Mom. See her for the first time in a long time. Don't look away. Force yourself to really look at her more closely. And as you move closer to her and really lean and see right in her eyes, you will notice something more.

As you gaze through her eyes you will almost feel her warmth and love. She is so deserving and so giving of love. Lean in and see it and feel it. Look past the eyes and begin to see her soul. She's so beautiful, isn't she?

And just being with her and connecting with her is so comforting, isn't it, Mom? She is the only person in this world that knows everything you are feeling, seeing, and thinking. In fact, she is the only person that has been there with you every step of the way. Remember her?

You two always worked so well together. You have gone through life together, through the highs and lows. When you were up she celebrated with you and gave you encouragement, and when you were down, you would have a heart to heart with each other.

Always together, through everything. So, what happened?

Have you forgotten this amazing person that you had shared your life with up until now?

She is the one constant in your life that has always been there for you no matter what. There is no getting rid of her. Wherever you go she goes and she is there with you. You just forgot about her, right?

She's still there. She is one of those friends that you don't need to talk to for years but when you do, you are right back where you left off.

It's time to reconnect and catch up with her. You two are a team and have an unbreakable bond. You trust and support one another and guide each other. You are stronger when you two are together.

Share with her, Mom. Be there for her. Give her a pep talk and let her know that you have her back. Remind her that you are a survivor, a warrior, and that you are ready to face any challenge.

Show her the determined and motivated individual you are. Put those shoulders back and stand tall before her. You are Mom. Ever so powerful.

And as you look at each other and finally see each other again, motivate one another, and begin to feel the oneness and strength that the two of you have when you are united. This will give you the positive assurance and energy you need to face the day.

Never, ever, will you pass by a reflection of this amazing woman without stopping and checking in. It will be your private meeting. Your personal discussion. Always check in and greet one another.

You love one another more than anything else in the world. Show that love. Respect one another and support and encourage one another.

And no matter what the day ahead brings, you know that at the end of it, you will be together again, ready to support and care for one another. And when you wake up tomorrow, you will be ready to take on the day together.

And when you do, watch out world. It is a force to be reckoned with.

It is Mom!

Chapter 12

I RECHARGE

Good Day, Mom.

I'm not sure what time you are reading this, if it is in the morning or at night. If it is morning, I could say, "Good Morning."

"Good Morning." What a nice sentiment. The thought would have the assumption that you had a good night. How presumptuous of me to say that then. For me to say, "Good Morning," I would have to have the impression that you are enjoying the morning, having awoken after a good night's sleep.

Sleep. Remember that, Mom? Remember when you were so tired you could just let your head hit the pillow and you were out for the night. Not a care in the world just the task at hand of sleeping.

Sure, when you were raising your child you had those sleepless nights when they would wake you. Maybe they needed to be fed, had a nightmare, or just weren't tired. But that was all part of being a Mom and I bet I'm right, you would love to go back in time and have those things keep you awake at night rather than what you are experiencing now.

Nothing compares to what keeps you awake now, does it, Mom? Even when it is all quiet and you know everyone is in a safe place and asleep for the night, that mind of yours just keeps going. There is no more going to sleep and having fun and happy dreams that you discuss in the morning.

Right now, sleep doesn't even seem like a part of your life. Even when you do fall asleep you awaken with the shock that you actually fell asleep. It is like you are in bed, on high alert at all times. There really is no deep sleep.

During the day, what you do now is more like a sleep walk, half awake, half asleep. You speak with low energy and you hear with less. You are a walking shell of a person as you continue in this nightmare. At night you may go to bed, and you may close your eyes, but your thoughts and your visions are so vivid, they keep the nightmare going 24/7.

Am I close, Mom?

I hope I'm not, but I bet I am pretty darn close.

Mom, your child is connected to you. They are a part of you. Remember that invisible force? Well, it knows no time. There is no night or day. Just now.

Your child is in their darkest storm, whether they know it or not, and you are right there being pummeled over and over by the tsunami sized waves.

Who can sleep during a time like this? Someone has to do something, even if it is just suffering.

Mom, I want to ask you a question. When your child was younger and at home, and they were due to come home at a certain time and they went way over the time, what did you do?

You worried, right? You watched the clock and paced and thought your horrible thoughts. You envisioned your child lost or harmed in some way, that they were in danger and that you needed to find them now. You called people, searched for them, and you were so angry that you may have even anxiously said, "when they get home I'm going to kill them." Humorous to think about now, but not at the time. You were in intense trauma.

Your thoughts and visions were so real in your mind that your body actual felt the events as if they were real.

You began to be stressed, anxious and your body released certain hormones. You may have begun to shake, sweat, and/or have other symptoms of your despair.

You had never been so scared in your life as you envisioned every horrible thought your mind could produce. You just wanted all your fears to go away and for your child to walk through that door.

Well, we all know how that story and many more after it ended. Your child finally came home!

Now, you either yelled and screamed for a while as you released all of your pent-up fears and anger, or you lovingly greeted them with a big hug, while you shared how worried and scared you were, never wanting to let them go.

Either way, your body went through a roller coaster ride of emotions and hormones, basically having a huge surge and ending with a crash. That wasn't easy on you. In fact, depending on the occurrence, if you were to describe it to someone right now, you probably would feel every emotion you felt at that time right here and now.

Shocks to our system have a way of staying with us our entire lives. We remember them like they happened yesterday. The events are so traumatic that all we have to do is call them up into our mind, and our body will react as if we are there again in real time.

This is why people do not like to talk about traumatic events. Their bodies relive the pain and fear even if it happened decades ago. The recall ignites the body. The mind is connected to the body.

Whether you are aware of it or not, you are in the same state you were when your child did not come home on time. That worry and fear is on high gear.

You are having thoughts and visions that are so real that your body is feeling them as if they were really happening. Even if your child is currently safe and sound somewhere, you don't know that, so you are filling your mind with where you think they may be and what may be happening. Just like before, you are envisioning them lost or harmed in some way, they are in danger and you need to save them now.

But it's different this time, isn't it? They can open doors and leave. They can drive cars or have friends pick them up. They are older and can to do what they want. Whatever the situation you are left without being able to control them and what they do.

The minute they leave is the minute your mind starts to fill in the blanks of where they are and what they are doing. Of course, you are not sleeping.

But here is the funny thing, Mom. Whether you sleep or not, whatever your child is doing, is going to happen. Your worrying is not going to change anything. You staying awake all night is not going to make the situation better.

There really is no reason for you not to have a good night's sleep. And there is only one thing keeping you from having it, and that is your mind.

Instead of worrying about what we cannot change, what if we trick your mind. What if we gave it a night off from worry and doubt and replaced it with something else? What if that thought was something that helped you sleep? Would you do it?

Mothers all over the world are lying awake worrying about their children. Mothers of soldiers or patients in hospitals, it doesn't matter, these Moms are filling their minds with make believe stories of the terrible things that could happen. In most cases, their worst scenarios never happen. It was all in the minds. And it is keeping their minds tarnished and their bodies sick.

Time to turn the channel.

Mom, when you go to bed tonight, when you are finally tucked in and relaxed, I want you to think about your child with their best friend. You know who they are because you remember them having so much fun together. They are both together today at their current age and they are laughing and happy. In your mind, your child is happy and joyous and they are having a great time. Pretend they are at camp or away on a holiday. They are having fun, in the water, on a boat, with other friends. They are happy and enjoying life.

Mom, I know it is hard to imagine, and you don't even have to think about this particular scenario. Pick one that works for you.

The point is that your mind, well it doesn't know the difference between a truth or a lie. Whatever you tell it, it will believe. It's your choice. It is so gullible, it will believe whatever you tell it.

You can tell it that your child is in danger, and your mind will instruct your body to release stress hormones and keep you awake so that you can become weaker and weaker.

Or you can tell it that your child is happy and having fun, enjoying their life right now and that they are in safe space, and your mind will instruct your body to relax, and to go to sleep.

It's your choice.

How do you want to be tomorrow morning? With a good night's sleep, you can feel refreshed and rejuvenated and at minimum be ready and have the energy to take on the day.

Without a good night sleep, you can continue your sleep walk, slowly depleting your body of the rest and regenerating it needs.

It's your choice.

Remember when your child was small and you used to read them beautiful bed time stories so that they could sleep easier and have sweet dreams. Those stories were always happy and insightful. You know how to do it, Mom. You did it for years.

What is your fairy tale that will help you go to sleep?

It's your choice, Mom. Just remember, it is all in your mind. You choose your thoughts. You choose your outcomes.

Your child is sleeping and they are recharging. Why not you?

Go to bed, Mom. Go when you are tired, go when you are not tired. It doesn't matter. Lie to your mind. Tell it whatever you want. The happier and brighter the thoughts, the better you will sleep.

Sleep, Mom. God knows you need it!

Now, once upon a time, there was this amazing Mom…………

Chapter 13

I SHARE

Hey, Mom.

I can't help but think about you as a child. You were so carefree, weren't you?

Did you have a childhood friend in your neighborhood? Do you remember them well? Maybe you are still in touch with them.

It's interesting how when you find a friend, you seem to have similar interests. Sometimes those similarities got in the way though. Remember when you liked something and then your friend bought it? Or someone got the Christmas gift you had asked for?

Having friends and neighbors close by is a wonderful, safe feeling. You always know there is someone near by if you need anything.

I bet right now, you can look around your neighborhood and you can see things and know things about people just from looking at their yards. There is the nicely manicured lawn from the retired gentleman, or the flower pots that the lady with the cats has down the street.

Maybe it's that family of five that has toys strewn across the yard. Or what about that single guy with the sports car?

Everyone gives away a little hint about themselves in their yards, balconies or driveways for the rest of the world to see. Everything else about these people is hidden inside their homes, tucked away nice and private for us to only guess what is happening behind those closed doors.

When you look around at your neighborhood, Mom, what do you think is behind those closed doors? Are you really concerned what people are doing or thinking right now? Probably not. You have more important things to think about other than what your neighbors are doing, right? So, why is it that so many of us care about what other people think? Are you wondering if people are thinking about you and your family?

Mom, are you tucked away nice and private in your home, keeping your dark secret about your child and their addiction away from everyone you know?

It's funny how we take on the emotion of shame when one of our children has an addiction. Your child is out there parading around for all to see with no thought about what people think. Why would you hide away in shame? It doesn't make any sense, does it? But we do. We hide in our homes hoping and praying that no one will find out. We all know that people will talk and put us and our family down. They will think less of us and treat us differently.

Is that how you are thinking? Mom, is it?

The truth of the matter is that it really doesn't matter what other people think. Most people don't think at all. They are not thinking about you and your situation because they don't know about it.

What is absolutely hilarious about the whole issue of hiding your child's addiction from the world is, most of the people around you are doing the exact same thing. Any person a stone's throw away from you is probably going through some sort of issue very similar to yours.

You are not alone!!

Addiction, whether to alcohol or drugs is so rampant, it is affecting everyone somehow, some way. You are not the only one!

Mom, when is the last time you shared your vulnerability about your situation with an acquaintance or a complete stranger? I guarantee that if you started opening up about your family and what they are going through, you will have more support and understanding than you think.

Sure, there will be those judgmental people that will use it against you. Remember, those people are already down and out and want to bring you down to their level. We don't have time for those people.

I'm talking about people that are suffering just like you, that you can talk with and share your situation. The more you open up about what you are going through, the more you will allow others around you to open up. They will begin to open their doors and come out from hiding in shame.

You just need to open your door. No more hiding, Mom. You did nothing wrong. You have nothing to be ashamed of. You are confident and strong and know that everything you do is to help your child.

Your child too has no reason to be ashamed. It is just the roulette wheel that landed on them to be selected for the addiction

You know this better than anyone because you have been going through this in your mind a thousand times. Examples of the luck of the draw have been around you your whole life.

Those guys that drove recklessly, smashed their cars and never got hurt. But the sweet innocent guy that chose to drive with them that night, ends up dying in the car crash.

The kids that tried different drugs recreationally and walked away from it unscathed. But that one person became addicted and couldn't stop using.

The students that partied every weekend getting drunk and then going to school on Monday with no repercussions. But that one person who continued to drink during the week.

The guy that robs a store and gets arrested. But his friend that just happened to be with him that night goes to jail too.

Luck of the draw, right. No one said it was fair. It just is.

The safest thing is to not be in the situation at all, but we know that it is not possible. Everyone wants to try things. It is the consequences that we have to learn to live with, isn't it, Mom?

So, here you are living the consequences of something that has happened to your child. Your child went out with one thing in mind, and came out with a different result. That's all it is.

Nothing for you to be ashamed of, nothing for anyone else to feel ashamed about either.

Strong, powerful Moms know, that they are stronger and more powerful when they support and help one another. What is better than one diligent Mom, but more strong Moms.

You, Mom, have a story. You are living something that is unfair and unimaginable. So are other Moms. You are not alone.

I want you to know that! You are not alone. There are many Moms out there right now, hiding alone in shame, doors closed.

Mom, won't you open up about yourself and your situation? Won't you help yourself and help other Moms by sharing your ordeal?

There is strength in numbers. You are stronger to fight the fight when there are more of you. What if you had an army to fight? What would you fight for? What changes would you want to see? Maybe, just maybe, you are the one that is supposed to ignite this change?

Are you willing to do that, Mom? Are you strong enough, confident enough, to take on this challenge? What changes could you see happening that would help you, your child, your neighborhood, and other Moms with their situation?

Mom, you are not alone. There are thousands of Moms just like you that feel helpless and are hiding away. Imagine if you took all of that negative energy and you put it towards something positive. What would that look like?

Mom, you can take this experience lying down, hiding in the shadows with your secret, or you can stand up and find your fellow Moms. Start by talking and sharing your story. Not with shame, not with judgment towards your child, but with the story of how you fell into this and how you are working your way out as a family.

You are a family in need of support and guidance. The only way for you to get the support you need is to first open up about it. Be vulnerable. Be human. Be able to ask for help.

Start with your doctor, or a clinic. Make some calls to support groups and online forums. Look for other Moms that are sharing your exact situation.

No more hiding. No more shame.

This isn't your event. It is your child's. You are just part of their experience. You don't own it, they do. You don't need to be ashamed. You did nothing wrong. No one did.

Find your tribe, Mom. They are out there. And they are looking for you too. They need you as much as you need them.

Open your door, take a step outside, and walk freely as the Mom with a child who has an addiction. Everything will seem so much different when you do.

I can see you now, stepping out with your head held high.

"Hey, look! There is that strong, confident Mom from down the street."

I see you, Mom! I see you!

Now, come find us!

I AM MOM

I am a caring, nurturing person

I am confident and determined

I attract all things positive

I am calm and understanding

I am willing to learn and grow

I love myself and others love me

I am respectful and others respect me

I accept my weaknesses and celebrate my strengths

I have peace of mind

I am in control of myself

I am not alone

I AM MOM

ABOUT THE AUTHOR

Dr. Fran Banting is a Holistic Life Coach and Mindfulness Expert and resides in British Columbia, Canada.

Dr. Banting earned her Doctorate in Philosophy specializing in Holistic Life Coaching and has been studying the mind and body connection for over 25 years. She has worked alongside some of the most prominent individuals in her field, including, the master of human behavior, Bob Proctor. She offers various coaching and counselling programs to individuals and corporations through her company, Dreampath Consulting.

To reach Dr. Banting, please visit www.dreampath.ca for contact information.